THE
FEEDBACK POCK

By Mike Pezet

Drawings by Phil Hailstone

"A straight-talking guide to creating a better understanding of the feedback process. Advocating awareness of the beliefs and values that underpin the joint feedback relationship, the critical skill of feedback is presented here with clarity, offering powerful, simple and effective tips."
David Harrison, Director, Kendal Specsavers

"Gives clear guidance on how to give feedback that improves performance, and provides an invaluable addition to any manager's toolkit. The book demonstrates how structured feedback significantly improves employee motivation and uses robust academic research to guide professional practice in a way that is stimulating and accessible."
Sue Gill, Lecturer in Business Management, Salford Business School

Management Pocketbooks Ltd
Laurel House, Station Approach, Alresford, Hants SO24 9JH, U.K.
Tel: +44 (0)1962 735573   Fax: +44 (0)1962 733637
E-mail: sales@pocketbook.co.uk
Website: www.pocketbook.co.uk

Class No.

8.99

Checked

This edition published 2010.

British Library Cataloguing-in-Publication Data – A catalogue record for this book is available
from the British Library.

ISBN 978 1 906610 12 8

Design, typesetting and graphics by **efex ltd**. Printed in U.K.

CONTENTS

DEDICATION
To Sue for all your belief
and to Hil, JP and Louis
for all your support and
encouragement.

INTRODUCTION

'My advice: Don't worry about yourself. Take care of those who work for you and you'll float to greatness on their achievements.'

HSM Burns
Former president, Shell Oil

FOOD FOR THOUGHT

The ability to give effective feedback has become one of the most critical management skills of recent years. Why?

One reason is cost. The economic downturn triggered by the banking collapse in 2008 has resulted in fierce competition and renewed focus on margin and profit. Many organisations have found that underperformance had gone unnoticed and unaddressed while the profits were rolling in. Underperformance means lost revenue, not to mention lost opportunities. A high standard of performance is not something that can be left to a yearly review. Frequent, ongoing feedback is essential.

Another reason for the relatively new prominence of feedback is the potential offered by the new generation entering the workforce. They bring competitive advantage because they understand how social networking and fast communication can solve problems and reach new markets. They **expect** to receive daily performance feedback.

INTRODUCTION

FOOD FOR THOUGHT

A CIPD study (2007) into British employees and their attitudes found, rather shockingly, that:

33% of employees considered they rarely or never got feedback on their performance

40% of employees felt their work didn't matter or was of little importance

What is the cost if a third of the workforce feels disenfranchised?

A study of 19,700 exit surveys by the Saratoga Institute (1997) found that:

- The percentage of employers who thought their people resigned mainly for money **89%**
- The percentage of employees who actually resigned for money **12%**

Lack of feedback and coaching to aid development was the third most cited reason for resignation. The first and second reasons were the job not matching the description or not being suitable for their skills.

WHO THIS BOOK IS FOR

This book is for managers, trainers and workers who understand the importance of feedback and want to develop their skills further. It is for all those who believe that feedback conversations are essential for engaging motivation, developing potential and building effective working relationships.

The book builds on the traditional view, which defines feedback as giving information about a person's performance. Feedback certainly is information about a person's performance, but it also encompasses a wide range of variables that affects the relationship, some of which **you** influence, as well as creating an 'impression' of what you meant and intended by your feedback.

Effective feedback requires you to take those variables into account, working with the recipient to form a feedback relationship that engages, minimises misinterpretation and increases acceptance.

INTRODUCTION

THE CASE FOR REGULAR FEEDBACK

Regular feedback is essential for effective learning and performance as it:
- Develops skills, ability, knowledge, experience, competence and confidence
- Reinforces desired behaviours
- Shifts perceptions

Regular feedback also:
- Reduces role anxiety and maintains focus by reassuring people they are performing as expected
- Demonstrates the organisation's belief that people are their best asset
- Forms a key building block in the relationship between manager and staff member
- Prevents self-regulation, when people interpret their jobs and priorities solely from their own frame of reference and not in conjunction with organisational goals and needs
- Meets high performers' need for information to help them develop and progress
- Prevents performance issues becoming performance problems

INHIBITING FACTORS

If regular feedback is essential to well-being, managing performance and growing capability, why, then, the lack of it? Here are some of the reasons I have encountered:

Personal beliefs
People's personal beliefs drive powerful arguments for not giving feedback, eg:

- *My team know when they're doing well; I only need to tell them when they are doing badly*
- *Too much praise will go to his/her head*
- *Giving feedback is a distraction from doing my job, besides that's what HR is for*

Lack of training and experience
Many are unclear about what to give feedback on and how to do it. Newly promoted managers, in particular, may either receive limited training in feedback skills or are assumed already to have the skills and end up 'guessing' how to give feedback.

INHIBITING FACTORS

Past experiences
Negative experiences of giving feedback, eg emotional reactions, misunderstandings or conflict, cause some managers to fear a repeat performance.

Cultural/Organisational norms
The organisation doesn't emphasise the value of regular feedback outside the yearly appraisal. Leaders don't model or encourage good practice.

Pressure
People are always under pressure to meet their targets. If the organisation doesn't promote regular feedback, then making time to develop staff through feedback or coaching can be seen as a distraction from the 'real' job.

POPULAR MISCONCEPTIONS

A frequent misconception I encounter is the belief that people will automatically respond appropriately to the type of feedback they are given. For example, people will be motivated by positive feedback, while negative feedback will demotivate or stop particular behaviour.

One of the reasons for this particular misconception is the mistaken belief that the person giving the feedback can control how it is interpreted by the receiver. A further influence lies in the 'genetics' of feedback literature. Early research, from which much of the popular literature derives, studied feedback through the lens of machinery. Positive feedback made things run, negative feedback made things stop. Those principles fitted nicely with the command and control managerial philosophy/literature from the early to middle stages of last century.

But people are not machines, so whether feedback is perceived as positive or negative will rest with the beholder and their values, beliefs and their experience of the situation and of you.

POPULAR MISCONCEPTIONS

Here is an example of a typical misconception.

> Sue's boss, Phil, normally only commented on her performance when things went wrong. But when he returned from a training course he said:
>
> *'Sue, I want you to know you've done a great job this week.'*
>
> Although the feedback was positive, Sue actually found it demotivating. She had done a lot of different activities and wanted to know **what** she had done well so it could be repeated. Despite asking for more detail, all she was given was the same generalised feedback.

No doubt the boss's intentions were good and if his feedback was positive then why should it demotivate? For Sue the lack of detail and reluctance to discuss what she **had done** made her feel she was on the receiving end of a technique from the training course rather than her contributions to the business genuinely being appreciated.

WHY FOCUS ON ENGAGEMENT?

The feedback Sue received didn't engage her. Engagement, as opposed to satisfaction, is where people feel appreciated and involved. Engaged people are prepared to go the extra mile for the organisation because they are focused and passionate about what they do.

The key factor influencing engagement with an organisation is the relationship people have with you, their manager. That relationship is affected by the shared ownership, quality and meaningfulness of the feedback conversations you have, or don't have. Genuine feedback demonstrates that you appreciate people, their situations, skills, aspirations and contributions. Appreciation is a key building block for engagement.

NATURE OF FEEDBACK

'Growth means change and change involves risk, stepping from the known to the unknown.'

George Shinn
American basketball coach

WHAT IS FEEDBACK?

Traditionally we were told that feedback about a person's performance needed to be judgement-free. The way in which we perceive events, though, means that feedback can never be entirely judgement-free, something we return to in chapter three. In addition to the influence of our perception, there are further variables that can create an impression other than the one you'd intended.

1. Noticeable variables
- The words and evidence used to compose your feedback
- Location of the feedback delivery, eg in public or private
- Formal frameworks you might use in your feedback, eg competencies
- Organisational systems, eg appraisals
- Formal outcomes of past discussions, eg goals, actions
- Prior agreement on boundaries of feedback

WHAT IS FEEDBACK?

There are less obvious elements that can also have a strong impact on the impression you create.

2. Shadowy variables
- Your conversational style, tone, gestures, etc
- The judgements you make to explain someone's performance
- The strength of the relationship and degree of trust between you
- Your disposition towards the person, history of feedback, what you generally notice in their performance (is it more what they do wrong or what they do well?)
- Your personal attitude towards feedback (are appraisals an inconvenience or an opportunity?)
- Wider cultural factors (are people expected to comply without question?)

WHO GIVES FEEDBACK?

Formal and informal feedback can come from a number of sources:

- From other people, peers, managers, friends, family

- From the job – eg instrumentation, statistics

- From the individual – people continually generate feedback about their own performance when they mentally critique and review the experience

APPROACHES TO FEEDBACK

Specific types of feedback, eg positive or negative, are covered in chapter four. However, feedback fits within three approaches:

- **Informal feedback** – a spontaneous part of everyday conversations, eg off the cuff comments, appreciative praise
- **Formal feedback** – deliberate observation of someone's performance within a structured discussion
- **Generative feedback** – a reciprocal exchange between giver and receiver, where all parties are open to generating personal and systems change as a result of the feedback

FEEDBACK CONVERSATIONS

The aim of this book is to encourage people jointly to design feedback relationships where feedback conversations, be they informal, formal or generative, are a regular and expected part of the working day or week. The book will help you:

- Understand that you have to start with yourself – your feedback will not be listened to and accepted until you have learned how to manage your own perceptions, distortions, etc
- Control the tendency to lay blame by understanding the effect that attributions (the assumptions you make) have on feedback
- Compose feedback that is of use and value
- Choose from a range of popular feedback techniques
- Have feedback conversations that engage and develop
- Support performance after a feedback conversation

A feedback relationship that is jointly designed will help you work **with, rather than against**, the dynamics that occur in feedback conversations, and will increase the likelihood that what you have to say is both listened to and accepted.

PERCEPTION

'We must always tell what we see.
Above all, and this is more difficult, we must always see what we see.'

Charles Peguy
French poet and essayist

OVERVIEW

People won't accept feedback if they don't believe it to be credible or accurate. If they won't accept it, to what degree, if any, has it been effective?

It's important to appreciate that the foundations of good feedback are the **judgements** you form as a consequence of what you observe, ie your perception. Misunderstandings largely result from differences in perception between the parties involved.

Use your eyes, ref!

Most people don't give their perception or its influence much thought. Indeed studies demonstrate that the majority of people assume everyone's perception is similar to their own.

PERCEPTION

OVERVIEW

Your perception is shaped by your unique experiences, needs, values and expectations. These influence and distort not only what you pay attention to, but also the stories you subliminally develop to form your judgements. Because of those unique distortions we all see the world differently. Yet many of us still feel perplexed when our colleagues see situations differently from ourselves!

By understanding some of those distortions, and learning to use some simple techniques, you will be able to reduce perceptual differences and consequently make your feedback more effective. To help you, this chapter will look at:

- The magnifying glass effect on your perception
- Inferences you use to add detail
- Attributions you make to explain why something happened
- Horns or halo
- Observer – Actor effect

THE MAGNIFYING GLASS

The first step for managing your perception is to acknowledge that it is inevitable you will distort not only what you see going on around you, but also the stories you'll develop to explain events.

One such distortion influences what captures your attention. It acts like a magnifying glass, concentrating your attention on distinctive features within a situation, namely people and their behaviour, while blurring your awareness of the impact of environmental influences.

The magnifying glass distortion means that people, and their actions, become the most prominent feature that you'll recall in your explanatory stories. The implication for feedback is that your judgement may be unbalanced, because in your recollection behaviour will be more important than environmental factors.

THE MAGNIFYING GLASS

Take this example.

Derek, a very competent manager, developed a directive style that captured people's attention. When his project fell behind on time and profit people perceived that it was caused by the effect of his management style. He was moved sideways and eventually left the company.

A later investigation found, however, that the conditions for failure were in place long before Derek joined the project. The initial negotiations to establish the terms of the contract were complex and had been inadequate.

But in reviewing the situation at the time, everybody had underestimated the effect of the environmental factors and focused their gossip and feedback on his personality and behaviour.

OTHER DISTORTIONS

Distortion of your perception also occurs through the explanations you make to account for situations. Like a detective, you'll piece together bits of information to build stories that explain what you see. The trouble is you're more akin to the amateur detective whose equipment is a bit skewed!

The equipment is skewed by manageable distortions such as inferences. **Inference** is the process of selectively filtering what you perceive in a situation in order to support the conclusions you have already formed.

INFERENCE – I KNOW I'M RIGHT!

Stories need detail to make them plausible and support your beliefs. One way you'll add detail to what you perceive is through making inferences. The main information you'll use for this is that vast collection of trusted knowledge and experience you have.

Consider your mind as a well-used computer hard drive; it's fast-ish and full of all sorts of essential software. Software such as experience, beliefs, values, needs, expectations, etc. So you look at a situation and add detail to build a story that fits your view of the world. The process is somewhat like a wonky calculator:

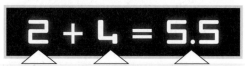

You gather information from your senses

You add your inbuilt beliefs, assumptions, etc

RESULT!
It doesn't quite reflect reality but it will certainly do for an explanation!

The trouble is that when unrestrained inferences become 'facts' or 'the truth' you undermine someone's perception of the accuracy of your feedback.

LADDER OF INFERENCE

EXAMPLE

You observe a partial picture of a situation
'I notice Tom, a new senior manager, frequently turns down social functions'

1

In the absence of other explanations you add detail to the picture by importing your beliefs
'I believe 'good' senior managers attend social functions'

2

And form a fresh belief
'Perhaps Tom is lacking as a senior manager'

3

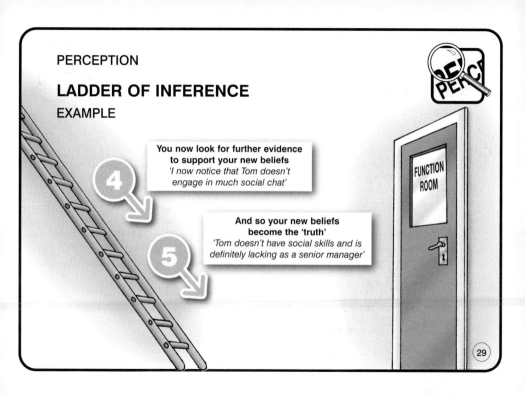

LADDER OF INFERENCE

EXAMPLE

The gossip led to people questioning Tom's suitability. His inability to attend social functions was a genuine problem for the company because senior managers were ambassadors for the organisation. However, those unchecked inferences became 'fact' and Tom received ambiguous and confusing feedback.

The situation changed when one manager decided to check the accuracy of the inferences. The manager became aware of two issues affecting Tom's performance. Firstly, he was providing intense personal care to his critically ill partner. Secondly, Tom believed that senior managers should not discuss their private lives. That belief prevented him from allowing people to appreciate his situation and give him support.

Once the actual, rather than inferred, problem was clarified and understood, a combination of feedback, constructive dialogue and problem solving enabled the company to work at a solution that suited both them and Tom.

ATTRIBUTIONS

Along with unrestrained inferences, your **attributions** also distort your perception. Attributions are the explanations you develop to account for what caused things to happen. When you make an attribution you'll blame the cause of events, or someone's behaviour, on either the person or the environment.

Like inferences, attributions are semi-conscious habits that everyone takes for granted. However, knowingly or not, your attributions can contain the seeds of blame and make people feel defensive in feedback situations.

One of the most beneficial actions you can take to increase the acceptance of your feedback, therefore, is to master the attributions you make. See the diagram on the next page.

PERCEPTION

ATTRIBUTION – HOW WE DO IT!

The diagram gives an idea of how you explain why a situation occurred.

You observe a situation or someone's behaviour

You believe the situation or behaviour was caused by

Internal cause	External cause
Some aspect in the person	Some aspect in the environment

You attach the cause to

A feature of the person
You believe the cause is a feature of the person such as:

- Skills, intellect, ability
- Beliefs
- Their background, etc

A feature of the environment
You believe the cause is a feature of the environment such as:

- The influence of other people, eg managers, peers, family
- Organisational factors, eg systems, structure, processes, budgets, hierarchy, culture
- Luck

ATTRIBUTION – HOW WE DO IT!

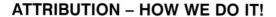

You consider the cause was

| Generally controllable by the person | Generally not controllable by the person |

The blame for causing the situation or behaviour is

On the person
They are largely to blame for what
happened

On external factors
The person is largely blameless for what
happened

EXAMPLES OF ATTRIBUTION

Here are some attributions you'll hear every day at work. See if any sound familiar:

- She succeeded because she thought ahead and anticipated what was required
- She succeeded because she had a lot of support

- He must be late for the meeting because of traffic problems
- He is always late for meetings because he's so disorganised

- He should have known better than to order those goods
- He had no choice; the department head told him to go ahead

- Who can blame her for being negative; the culture in that whole department is negative
- She should change her attitude and stop being so negative, it's bringing everyone else down

- Lucky he was in the right place at the right time
- He worked hard to get that promotion

What causes are being blamed? Where does control of the cause lie in each example?
How do you think a recipient might react if these were feedback statements?

HORNS OR HALO

Your attributions are also influenced by the horns or halo you give a person. These are biases that need to be managed.

- **Horns effect** – Arises from your negative conclusions about someone; perhaps you dislike or have a low opinion of them. You will look for evidence to maintain your attributions and support your feelings. For example, you notice what someone does wrong before seeing what they do well

- **Halo effect** – Arises from your positive feelings about someone; your attributions will continue to support those feelings. For example, you will pay attention to what they do well in order to support your attribution that they're a 'good person'

To persuade you to change either type of attribution/belief you need to be presented or confronted with overwhelming evidence. In fact, you will put a great deal of effort into maintaining your attribution.

DEVELOPING YOUR SKILLS

You make attributions all the time because they help you simplify complex interactions and decisions about how you should act. One way to master your attributions is to follow Benjamin Franklin's advice and, 'Observe all men, **thyself most**'. Observing your attributions can increase your awareness and help you to identify your predispositions.

Simply spend ten or fifteen minutes observing situations and interactions around you. Try to be sensitive to the stories you're using to explain what's going on.

- What did you notice about your attributions to explain events?
- Did you make attributions about the control of the cause? For example, did you think it was a feature of the person and so controllable by them?
- What effect would your attributions have on your feedback?

THE BLAME GAME

One of the reasons blame manifests in attributions is because the magnifying glass effect encourages you to believe that personal/internal factors, such as attitude or skills, are the most likely explanation for events, rather than external/environmental factors. The more an outcome affects you personally, the more you will attribute the cause to personal factors.

Remember Derek? People's attributions, horns effect, 'blamed' his personality and behaviour. They failed to account for the effect of a contract he had had no involvement with. In addition, no one looked at Derek's manager's role and how well she managed and supported Derek.

Thinking back to the questions on the previous page, did you notice any bias in your attributions, ie did you more often pick environmental or internal causes? How sensitive were you to any environmental factors that may have been influencing people's behaviour? Environmental influences are always there; you just need to give a situation more consideration than you're used to and be prepared to look at your own role in creating the situation.

OBSERVER – ACTOR EFFECT

> *'Every truth has two sides.*
> *It is well to look at both before we commit ourselves to either side.'* **Aesop**

People fight for and defend what they consider to be the truth but, as Aesop highlights, there are different versions of the 'truth'. Indeed, your attributions are your version of the truth.

However apparent, truths are heavily distorted by a phenomenon called Observer – Actor Effect (Jones et al, 1965). The main feature of this is that generally when people share the same situation but occupy different roles, they will attribute different reasons for why things occurred.

Your attributions will be swayed by whether you're a participant (actor) in a situation or an observer, and whether the outcome has been positive or negative.

OBSERVER – ACTOR EFFECT

No matter which role you inhabit within a situation, the Observer – Actor Effect has a profound impact on what you believe is the true representation of events. When people are participants (actors), they generally believe they are reacting to **events**, therefore not directly responsible for what happens. At the same time, when people are observers, they believe others are **in control of their behaviour**, therefore responsible and accountable for events.

The perceived accuracy of any feedback you give will depend on your role in a situation and also the horns/halo effect. In addition Observer – Actor Effect makes you critical of others' performance and lenient with regard to your own.

The table overleaf gives an insight into how the 'truth' varies according to your role in a situation.

OBSERVER – ACTOR EFFECT

	When an outcome is positive	**When an outcome is negative**
When you are the observer you attribute the outcome to:	**Circumstances (external causes) made it a success** Lucky them! You believe environmental features were the cause, eg they had good resources, timely support, a good team or were just lucky	**Their skill/attitude/personality (internal causes) made it a failure** Blame time! You believe their personal features were the cause, eg they were disorganised, failed to communicate, had a poor attitude or didn't manage their team
When you are the actor (participant) you attribute the outcome to:	**My skill/attitude/personality (internal causes) made it a success** Praise me please! You believe success was largely due to your actions: your skills made the difference, you worked hard, your timely interventions were pivotal to success	**Circumstances (external causes) made it a failure** Don't blame me, it wasn't my fault! You believe uncontrollable environmental features were largely responsible: insufficient resources, little support, inadequate briefing, unrealistic targets

OBSERVER – ACTOR EFFECT

CONSIDERATIONS

Here are some points about Observer – Actor Effect:

- It can make you overlook someone's contribution to a successful outcome, so people may feel you don't recognise or reward their efforts

- In negative situations your feedback will be different from how they remember the situation

- People will defend their version of events because that is what they remember

- People will feel blamed for a negative outcome

- The horns/halo effect skews your perception. You look for evidence to maintain your belief: *'I told you so!'* Horns/halo means someone you like will get the benefit of the doubt more than someone you dislike

- Each party will see different problems in the same situation – problem solving and dialogue can therefore be difficult

ATTRIBUTIONS: SUMMARY

Attributions are essential for simplifying complex interactions. However, those spur-of-the-moment, unchecked attributions mean you can overlook personal qualities or situational factors. Without balance your attributions and feedback can cause misunderstanding and hurt. Consequently opportunities to improve performance, reinforce good practice or even address wider organisational issues can be missed.

With a little effort you can use the following technique to reap big dividends by managing your attributions to develop more engaging and effective feedback.

PERCEPTION

MANAGING YOUR ATTRIBUTIONS

In a controlled study of attributions in feedback situations*, one group of people (the test group) were encouraged to ask themselves a specific question before giving feedback, namely: *'What are all the possible causes for this situation and for this person's behaviour?'*

The other group, the control group, carried on assessing situations and giving feedback as normal. During the period of the study, 81% of the people in the control group reinforced or strengthened their view that the person was at fault for the situation or behaviour they were assessing.

In the same study, 68% of those asking the question (the test group) changed their attribution from believing that the person caused the outcome to environmental factors being responsible. The ensuing type of feedback, together with a problem solving approach, was reflected by the type of attribution they had formed.

So before composing feedback, simply ask yourself that same question. You will find that your awareness of other potential causes increases. And the more you practise the better you get!

* For further reference see http://www.feedbacktoolkit.com

MANAGING YOUR PERCEPTION

This chapter began with the statement that people don't accept feedback they believe isn't credible or accurate. As you've read, the magnifying glass, inferences and attributions combine to have a profound effect on what you perceive and believe to be the truth.

To increase the probability that your feedback will be accurate and therefore accepted, you must manage your perceptual distortions **before** you build your feedback for someone. The following acronym, **SOLD**, can help you build feedback that considers a wider range of influences than you may initially have accounted for.

S low down the speed of your conclusions – use the question on the previous page
O bserve the situation
L ook for possible alternative causes of behaviour – consider both internal and external
D isengage your bias; check your assumptions and attributions

You can now look towards composing feedback that will be engaging and useful.

COMPOSING FEEDBACK

'First learn the meaning of what you say, and then speak.'

Epictetus
Greek philosopher

OVERVIEW

Having formed your judgement of what has taken place, you now need to construct the content of your feedback, remembering to keep it clear and accurate.

Fedor (1991) identified that, post feedback, people have three general ways of reacting:

1. Using **feedback-seeking behaviours** – where they expend energy trying to clarify what you meant by your feedback and behaviour; can deteriorate into gossip.

2. Using **impression management behaviour** – where people, depending on whether your feedback was favourable or not, expend energy boosting or protecting their image.

3. Using the feedback to drive **performance behaviour**, which is what you want to happen.

COMPOSING FEEDBACK

OVERVIEW

If you want your feedback to encourage performance behaviours then it needs to be of value to the person by being accurate, useful and specific. This chapter will look at three factors that affect how closely it adheres to these qualities:

- Your **credibility**, which influences and underpins the value people place on your feedback

- The **language** you use, particularly adjectives, because they affect the clarity and accuracy of your feedback

- Use of the terms **positive and negative**. They help turn observations into feedback but also limit its usefulness

CREDIBILITY

Credibility, yours included, has a momentous influence on the acceptance of feedback. If you are perceived as credible then your feedback, even if negative, will be more readily considered because people trust your underlying motives.

Numerous studies have defined credibility but, consistently, people judge it by:

- **Expertise** – your familiarity with and knowledge of what their work entails, your qualifications, your weight of relevant experience, etc

- **Trust** – the strength of the relationship between you, how reliable your intentions are towards the person, ie do you help their performance and development or do you act as judge?

COMPOSING FEEDBACK

LOSING CREDIBILITY

Take this example of the link between manager, employee, credibility and value.

> Allie was a proactive, proud member of a flourishing hotel where customers were warmly welcomed and looked after.
>
> A new general manager took over the hotel. She immediately focused attention on what wasn't working but barely acknowledged, or reinforced, what Allie and the others were doing well. Within a month people felt under-appreciated, and energy was channelled into feedback-seeking behaviours such as backroom gossip. As the manager's credibility deteriorated, her feedback lost meaning and value and she had to resort to threats to motivate performance. Consequently, half of that motivated management team had resigned within two months.
>
> As Allie said, *'The new manager looked, but she didn't see'.*

BUILDING CREDIBILITY

The value placed on that manager's feedback, as well as the acceptance of it, was underpinned by the team's perception of her credibility. Credibility is as much built on daily interactions as it is on reputation. Reputations take time to build, but daily actions like the following cost little:

- Be clear about your purpose as a manager – are you a helper or a judge?
- Ask your people what they want feedback on, how often, what kind of feedback works for them, what it is they want to develop. Then work together to set targets and developmental goals
- Notice what people do well, offer spontaneous feedback that reinforces and praises
- Show you appreciate people's situations by recognising the challenges they face in the work they do
- Don't confuse directing with feedback. Feedback is your observation of someone's performance. Some managers, though, use feedback to suggest what to do, and if they don't get the response they really wanted, they resort to telling. Be honest from the beginning; if you want something done in a specific way don't confuse things by dressing it up as feedback

CLARITY OF LANGUAGE

To use your feedback, people have got to be able to convert it into useable knowledge. For that to happen, your feedback needs to be clear, understandable and accurate.

The words you use, particularly adjectives, can make your feedback seem subjective. Adjectives are a habitual part of communication. They quickly trip off the tongue without much effort because they capture and convey your impressions and feelings.

If you are careless in your use of adjectives, you run the risk of diverting the discussion away from evidence-based, factual content to opinions that are open to interpretation, things like motives, attitudes and values. The result is that people will question your accuracy, paving the way to disagreement.

USE OF ADJECTIVES

Here is an example of the effect of imprecise language in a yearly appraisal.

> Julia, a loyal employee, felt she had reached a plateau in her development. In her appraisal she wanted guidance and feedback from her boss, but despite repeated requests he avoided feedback until finally blurting out:
>
> *'Your pessimistic attitude stops you getting opportunities!'*
>
> The boss's message was blatantly clear, but the actual feedback was not. Julia was confused. What behaviours had created such a strong impression? How long had the boss held this opinion? Was she seen as a pessimist all the time, and by whom? Why hadn't he said anything before? To Julia the feedback was not only unclear but also, in her eyes, inaccurate and therefore wrong.

USE OF ADJECTIVES

The adjective used by Julia's boss, *pessimistic*, didn't describe actual behaviour but his opinion of a subjective issue – her attitude. Julia would be far more likely to argue (openly or silently) with his choice of word than hear the genuine feedback he was trying to convey.

Adjectives **label** people by attributing qualities that may or may not be accurate. This is critical because perceived accuracy is a threshold to acceptance, just as perceived inaccuracy undermines perception of your credibility.

DESCRIBING BEHAVIOUR

How could Julia's boss have conveyed his message without using a judgemental adjective? A good technique is to prepare and collect evidence before giving feedback, particularly when emotional about the subject. Another is simply to pause before speaking. Perhaps if he'd prepared or paused he might have said:

'At the last three team meetings you have been sitting on the outer edge of the group, looking out of the window. When you have contributed to the meeting it has been solely in the form of opinions on why the company is not as good as it used to be.'

He could also have invested time and effort to develop his skills in describing behaviour so that he was performing, rather than merely coping, during the appraisal. Better still, he could also have worked with Julia to establish a feedback relationship they both owned; regular incremental feedback is better than unexpected surprises.

COMPOSING FEEDBACK

DESCRIBING BEHAVIOUR

Feedback built on descriptions of behaviour

Is more accurate
Is easier to convert and use
Has less potential for misunderstanding

Observed behaviour
Interactions
Skills

Motives
Attitudes
Values

Feedback built on adjectives describing the person

Is potentially less accurate
Can be harder to transform and use
Increases potential for misunderstanding
Undermines credibility

COMPOSING FEEDBACK

DESCRIBING BEHAVIOUR: OBSERVATION

Describing behaviour takes practice. An easy way to develop your skills is through observing situations, for example interactions in a café. Here is an approach you could use:

1. In a café, or similar public place, observe the way people are being served.

2. Note the language and adjectives you say to yourself, for example, *'he served the customer cheerfully'* or *'she didn't seem to care for the customer'*. Check how clear your feedback is; would it actually help reinforce or improve their performance?

3. Spend some time identifying the behaviour that created those impressions. For example, *'he served the customer cheerfully'* could be described as, *'when the customer first arrived he made eye contact and smiled as he asked how he could help'*.

4. Compare the difference.

You will find that as your skills develop you will become less dependent on adjectives, instead describing actual behaviours. In particular, it will become easier to describe non-effective behaviours without implying blame.

COMPOSING FEEDBACK

POSITIVE & NEGATIVE FEEDBACK

While focusing on behaviour helps increase accuracy, another key area to consider is the usefulness of your feedback. To convert observations into useable feedback people generally, employ a positive and negative framework, where:

- Negative feedback conveys dissatisfaction with the person's performance
- Positive feedback conveys approval of the person's performance

The terms are familiar, easy to use and give an easy criterion for labelling what you see, ie actions are good or bad.

POSITIVE & NEGATIVE FEEDBACK

The terms positive and negative fulfil a useful purpose. They focus your perception and structure what you see, but they'll also inadvertently undermine the very thing you're trying to achieve, which is helping people perform.

The terms encourage you to perceive events in simple terms, ie things are either good or bad. This means you can miss a key feature of performance, namely that people act as a result of decisions made in dynamic situations. Your feedback can miss the point that people were doing the best they could **at that time**.

COMPOSING FEEDBACK

POSITIVE & NEGATIVE FEEDBACK

Positive and negative feedback focuses your attention on outcomes, which does have advantages. For example, positive feedback on a success gives people a glow of recognition; also, outcomes are easy to see and easy to measure. But the usefulness of outcome feedback is limited, as these typical examples of positive outcome feedback show:

- *'You did a really good job'*
- *'I thought that was a great success'*
- *'You did as well as Ben on that one'*
- *'That was as good a presentation as I could have given'*

The drawbacks are:

- It is easy to give generalised feedback because success and failure are obvious
- It doesn't isolate **what** people did to reach the outcome
- It doesn't indicate which behaviours to maintain, refine, improve or alter to improve performance

PROCESS FEEDBACK

For performance to develop, people need **process feedback**. Process feedback focuses on **how** someone went about doing their job. It helps people know **what** they did to reach the outcome.

McAfee et al (1995) found people placed more value on the combination of outcome and process feedback than outcome feedback on its own because it enabled higher levels of problem solving and performance.

OUTCOME & PROCESS FEEDBACK

Observing what someone does, the **process**, will reward people with feedback that helps develop their performance. You'll also find that when you compose process feedback, your feedback automatically becomes specific, which is of use to people because it is clear.

By combining improved skills in managing your perception (chapter three) with your knowledge of the effects of credibility and language, you are in a better position to know, rather than guess, the type of feedback that will be of value to the person.

The following pages have a range of actual examples of feedback in different settings and suggestions for improvement.

COMPOSING FEEDBACK

OUTCOME & PROCESS FEEDBACK
EXAMPLES

'You were a great help in that meeting'

Which might have been:

'During the meeting it was appreciated when you stepped in to answer some of the more difficult questions from the client. You spoke clearly, did not rush your answers, admitted when you didn't know something and responded by telling them when you would get back to them with answers. Those actions directly contributed to the success of the meeting and building a trusting relationship with the client.'

'I couldn't see a thing when you used the flipchart'

Which might have been:

'When you wrote on the flipchart the writing was a bit small. Occasionally you stepped in front of the board, so I couldn't see what was written because the flipchart was placed at an awkward angle to this side of the room.'

OUTCOME & PROCESS FEEDBACK
EXAMPLES

'Your presentation was so dull'

Which might have been:

'The presentation ran for a long time – there was a lot of information contained in it. For example the first six slides each contained ten lots of statistics, which required high levels of concentration to understand what was written, which in turn distracted me from hearing what you were saying.'

'You'd be a good match for this client because you're direct'

Which might have been:

'You are direct, by which I mean you are not afraid to put your opinion forward. When you do so, I notice that what you say appears to be accepted and appreciated by the person you are talking to. I can only assume you spend time being thoughtful about the person you are going to speak to.'

COMPOSING FEEDBACK

OUTCOME & PROCESS FEEDBACK
EXAMPLES

> *'Well done, you were a good chair in that meeting'*

Which might have been:

'You were a good chair in that meeting. You helped keep things on track when you intervened to ask people to clarify their points. On one occasion a particular person was dominating the discussion by raising her voice. You managed that situation by giving her your full attention, speaking in a calm voice and asking her to clarify the specific issue so we could help her.'

> *'Yes, the job you did with the vans was OK'*

Which might have been:

'You did three of the five vans to a very high standard. You paid attention to detail areas such as ensuring that the cab and exterior were clean for the customer. The other two did not meet that standard – the customer arrived to find rubbish under the seats and oily handprints over the bonnet and doors.'

COMPOSING FEEDBACK

COMPARATIVE & EVALUATIVE FEEDBACK

The further feedback styles, comparative and evaluative, which are primarily associated with outcome feedback, can be useful when used with care.

- **Comparative feedback** compares someone to another person or to a standard. Saying, *'You did as well as Ben'* compares their performance and its outcome to Ben's performance. The strength of comparative feedback is in giving someone a clear, concrete example or model of how to do things

- **Evaluative feedback** uses some form of value or judgement to appraise performance. For example, *'I thought that was a great success'* gives a measure to the outcome. The strength of evaluative feedback is in giving someone a measure between their current level and a desired standard, but as in that example it can be unclear what the speaker's measure of success is

Like process feedback, comparative and evaluative feedback is effective when it is of value and use to the recipient. However, inadvertent use of highly subjective standards in comparative feedback can cause misunderstanding and lack of acceptance.

COMPARATIVE & EVALUATIVE FEEDBACK

EXAMPLE

Greg wanted to know how to move forward in the company and received the following feedback from his boss:

'You need to get alongside me to find the opportunities. In fact you need to be more like Sanjoy, he is always badgering me and asking for new challenges.'

The intention had been to help, but in Greg's eyes Sanjoy lacked credibility because he was an aggressive manager with a very different attitude to work. Greg struggled with accepting the comparison because it neglected the qualities he brought to the business while elevating and valuing those of a manager he didn't respect or find credible.

Greg might have found the feedback more useful and acceptable if his boss had offered feedback on the qualities that Greg brought to the business along with clarifying the aspects of Sanjoy's approach that were of benefit.

COMPARATIVE & EVALUATIVE FEEDBACK

Some ways in which you can make comparative and evaluative feedback useful are:

- **Using measures or comparators that have credibility** – robust 360 or appraisal instruments that help performance in the workplace (some instruments can be too abstract)

- **Being precise** – you need to be clear about the skills you want them to develop: is it task skills, learning skills or relationship-building skills? What type of feedback will be most appropriate for the person and the skills being developed? For example, comparative feedback using observation and competencies might give people a clearer sense of direction than pass/fail evaluative feedback

- **By remembering to highlight their qualities** – comparing, or telling, them to be like another person, without explaining why you've used that comparison can be demotivating because it neglects their qualities

- **By recognising when you are using subjective standards** – we can unconsciously use subjective standards like values, attitudes etc without realising our feedback is unclear or perhaps difficult to understand. Recognise you are doing so and be prepared to clarify any areas of ambiguity

MAKING FEEDBACK EFFECTIVE

Here are some ideas for how you can make each type of feedback effective:

	Outcome feedback		Process feedback
	Comparative	**Evaluative**	
Objective measures	Compare them to competencies	Evaluate against agreed goals	What did they do to reach the outcome?
	Compare to other people who are credible in the specific area you want to develop performance	Evaluate against past appraisal actions	What behaviours were used?
		Evaluate against organisational standards that are clear	Who did they interact with?
	Compare to objective historical data		What decisions did they make along the way?
			How did you see them approach the task/learning/relationship?
Subjective measures	If you use measures such as your values, attitudes, what you would have done, people you admire, be aware that it may make your feedback ambiguous and open to interpretation. Therefore allow people the opportunity to question and clarify.		

SUMMARY

To encourage performance and reduce the potential for impression management or feedback-seeking strategies:

Make feedback of value

- Know what they want feedback on by forming a feedback relationship
- Link the feedback to their development needs and goals
- Be clear and genuine in your motives, be mindful of your credibility
- Prepare and pause before delivering your feedback

SUMMARY (CONT'D)

Make feedback accurate and useful
- Reduce ambiguity by managing your attributions
- Consider the impact of adjectives, describe behaviour rather than motives

Make feedback specific
- Be clear about what is being developed: task, learning or relationship-building skills
- Use comparative and evaluative feedback considerately to motivate performance
- Pay attention to **how** people do their job, not just outcomes, using process feedback to describe the behaviour used to reach the outcome

Decide for yourself; are you a developer of performance or a judge of performance?

FEEDBACK FRAMEWORKS

'Education is learning what you didn't even know you didn't know.'

Daniel J. Boorstin
American historian and writer

OVERVIEW

This chapter contains a range of techniques for giving feedback. No matter which technique you use, you should always focus on making your feedback **useful**, **accurate** and **specific** in order to encourage acceptance. Acceptance can also be affected by situations that cause someone to lose face or feel embarrassed, which we look at further in the next chapter.

The settings for the frameworks that follow range from one to ones, groups, workplace and training situations. Some are situation specific, whilst others are for more general use.

FEEDBACK FRAMEWORKS

CREATE A FEEDBACK CONTRACT

If you want to build effective feedback relationships then talk to people. Identify and establish what feedback works for them, discuss how they like feedback to be given. This gives people a sense of control and ownership and creates the conditions for high acceptance because the feedback will be relevant. In addition you'll know, rather than guess, what style and approach of feedback is appreciated.

Questions to ask
To set up an ongoing feedback relationship, some simple questions you can use are:
- What does a feedback conversation mean to you?
- What makes you want to use feedback? What turns you off feedback?
- What goals, skills etc do you want the feedback to help you achieve?
- How frequently do you want feedback conversations; formal or informal?
- What if I spot some performance 'problems': how do you want that feedback given?
- How do you like to get praise?

FEEDBACK SANDWICH

The first technique, the feedback sandwich, is very well-known. Negative feedback is given between two pieces of positive feedback, ie positive, negative, and positive.

✅ Pros

Gives your feedback structure, useful for building confidence when first learning to give feedback.

❌ Cons

People eventually become conditioned to the structure and anticipate the negative, undervalue the positives and attribute motives for the feedback, ie *'they always dress it up when they have something bad to say'*.

FEEDBACK FRAMEWORKS

STOP, START & CONTINUE

Feedback, verbal or written, is given on something you want someone to **stop** doing, **start** doing and **continue** doing.

 Pros

Quick structure, useful if time is short, gives a forward focus to the feedback. Good for use with groups where trust is at a good level.

 Cons

Stop, start can be seen as double negatives.

Option: use visual representations such as traffic lights as categories.

FEEDBACK FRAMEWORKS

ENQUIRY

Ask for their perspective of a situation/performance before offering your feedback.

 Pros

Potential for loss of face is reduced.
Gain insight into their perception
and measure of performance.
People feel respected and valued,
which builds a foundation for
developmental relationships.

 Cons

Unless you make your intentions
clear, people can be suspicious
as to why you want to get their
perspective first and consequently
they won't listen to the
conversation.

High levels of self-management are needed to listen and to control your attributions,
particularly if you hear something you disagree with.

FEEDBACK FRAMEWORKS

CURIOSITY/ENQUIRY

This is a general method with no set structure other than asking, *'when you did X I didn't quite understand what your intentions were?'* If the relationship has a good foundation of trust and security, then people perceive that the enquiry is about exploring and helping rather than blaming.

 Pros

Good when the relationship has strong foundations. Enables dialogue to consider the intended outcomes and explore alternative approaches.

 Cons

Can be perceived as a lead in to blame if people are insecure with you.

FEEDBACK FRAMEWORKS

THIS IS HOW YOU AFFECT ME

Feedback is used to raise the person's awareness of your reaction to their behaviour. The typical structure is:

Behaviour – When you did X behaviour: *'When you talked over the top of me'*
Effect – I felt X: *'I felt undermined'*

 Pros

It presents an undeniable consequence, your reaction. If delivered with minimal judgement (blame) it can be a powerful method for raising awareness and developing relationships. You can also follow the feedback with directions, eg *'you could instead do X.'*

 Cons

People can react defensively and dismiss your feedback, eg *'you didn't feel like that'*, which, unless you manage your reaction, can become an adversarial negotiation over who is right rather than learning from the feedback.

THE QUALITIES JUST UNDER THE SURFACE

Feedback is given both on visible qualities and the latent potential that could be realised through awareness.

 Pros

Appreciative and respectful of people. Contains reinforcing and forward-focused feedback. It is energising to hear about one's potential.

 Cons

Need to encourage people to follow up on generalised comments after the session to gain more detail and insight.

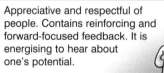

DISCLOSURE

People present responses to statements such as: 'my leadership strengths', 'my proudest moment', 'me at my best', 'me at my worst', etc. After hearing people's disclosure you give your feedback on the areas covered. Typically used with groups, but can also be used in one to ones or appraisals.

✓ Pros

Informative, gives insight, develops new understanding of people. Builds trust, strengthens relationships.

✗ Cons

Needs clear boundaries, ie don't disclose what you want kept private. Challenging for those who don't like presenting or self-disclosure. Some national cultures can be reluctant to take part because they keep their personal and business lives separate.

FEEDBACK FRAMEWORKS

CRITICAL INCIDENT

People select a critical incident to present and explore. They can explain what they were trying to achieve in that situation, the outcomes, and what they want feedback on.

 Pros

High degree of ownership and potential acceptance because people are receiving feedback on the areas they want to explore.

 Cons

May require time and high-level questioning skills to help move the conversation beyond the superficial.

FEEDBACK FRAMEWORKS

GIFT

Similar to secret Santa and suitable for groups. Everyone buys a gift that represents their named person (you can set guidelines, eg no more than £2.00 and second-hand). In turn they present their gift and explain how it represents the person.

 Pros

Fun, energising. Potentially high levels of acceptance because the vehicle for feedback is non-threatening.

 Cons

Some may resent the time needed to choose something.
Should not be used in groups with poor levels of trust.

One way to help build trust is to invest time and energy in establishing genuine feedback contracts that are appropriate to the situation, as described on page 73.

FEEDBACK FRAMEWORKS

NO NAME

People write feedback for a nominated person (names from a hat). They describe that person and what they are capable of without using their name or gender. People read the description, and as a group, guess who it is.

 Pros

Fun because of the mystery element. Can generate lots of secondary feedback as people guess. Pushes people to look in more detail at the other person.

 Cons

May need some form of guidance, eg describe three qualities you admire about how they work in the team.

FEEDBACK FRAMEWORKS

PRO

Present, Response and Ownership (PRO) is a three-stage performance management technique. **Present** means presenting your feedback and supporting evidence in a concise and clear manner in two or three sentences. **Response** means controlling yourself while they react. **Ownership** means using coaching techniques to generate ownership for the issue.

 Pros

Helps you clarify and present the issue clearly and concisely. Gives a framework to manage your own behaviour and a direction to progress the conversation.

 Cons

Confrontational, challenging. Can change a relationship from developmental to transactional. Use as an intervention or wake up call when performance is consistently not to the required standards.

PRAISE

Praise is needed but different people respond to different things. People might like to have appreciated and acknowledged:

- The originality of their ideas
- The value their critical thinking skills bring to the business
- Their drive and competence to make things 'happen'
- Their uniqueness
- Their quiet contribution
- The extra effort they make

Praise isn't just a simple *well done*. Praise is you acknowledging, through detailed feedback, that you recognise the qualities they bring, and how those qualities work for the business.

METAPHOR OR ANALOGY

Together with the remaining techniques in the chapter, this framework is more geared to training situations.

People convey feedback through imagery or stories, eg an animal or superhero, which encapsulates them or another person. Discussion and exploration of the metaphor are the key here. This approach is often used in team development, for example: *'Describe this team as a car, the part each person is and the roles you fulfil'*.

 Pros

Fun way to access feedback, creative element helps reveal new insights, opinions.

 Cons

Flippancy if not set up well. Based on comparative feedback, so people may react to the comparison (however the comparison is a representation of how they are seen, which is not necessarily who they are).

HOT SEAT

One person at a time receives feedback from every other member of the group.

✓ Pros

Large volumes of feedback can be given and received. Can be a cathartic, enabling process for groups that face issues, yet have high levels of trust and interpersonal skills.

✗ Cons

Potential for loss of face and non acceptance unless set up well. The process can cross personal boundaries and generate unintended momentum. That is because after each piece of feedback the next person can feel compelled to give 'better', more 'quality' feedback than the previous person.

COCKTAIL PARTY

People circulate as at a party, select a partner, give and then receive two or so minutes of feedback. A time-keeper moves people on to new partners, encouraging pairing up with people they have not had much contact with.

 Pros

Rapid way of sharing feedback. Potential loss of face reduced as people have a high degree of control by choosing who they initially talk to and the depth of the conversation. Process also allows people to clarify feedback through dialogue.

 Cons

Can become generalised or superficial if people lack focus or purpose for giving the feedback or if people feel insecure in the group.

FEEDBACK FRAMEWORKS

ASK FOR FEEDBACK

People request, either verbally or on a poster, the areas they wish to get feedback on. People give feedback via post-it notes. People gain further clarity through follow up conversations.

 Pros

Can give people a focus for their feedback and permission to give it. Loss of face is minimal because people are asking for feedback on areas they want clarity on. High level of ownership and acceptance.

 Cons

Can become generalised, (eg *'give me feedback on anything'*) when the feedback is not given a focus (eg on specific leadership qualities) and when asking for feedback is relatively new to people.

WHIRLWIND/SPEED FEEDBACK

Speed dating feedback. People sit in two columns of chairs, pairs facing each other. One column gives 30 seconds of feedback to their partner, repeated by feedback from the other person. Everyone moves one chair to their right or left – and repeat until everyone receives feedback. People gain further clarity through follow up conversations.

 Pros

Fast, high energy, spontaneous. Good with teams or groups that have high level of trust and themes to guide the feedback.

 Cons

Limited time to explore the feedback and understand the behaviour underpinning any adjectives, hence follow up required. Impulsive feedback may not be appropriate.

CONSTRUCTIVE FEEDBACK CONVERSATIONS

'If you want me to change I'll come around quicker if you treat me nice than if you treat me bad.' **Anon**

CONSTRUCTIVE FEEDBACK CONVERSATIONS

OVERVIEW

There may be occasions when you think you need to influence performance with 'negative' or 'critical' feedback. However, people who receive little or no performance feedback can be surprised when they suddenly receive feedback contrary to what they believe. Big shocks don't do anyone any favours. Performance should be developed incrementally; feedback, critical or otherwise, should be regular and agreed as a contracted part of your relationship.

But research of managerial practices indicates that regular, meaningful feedback is the exception rather than the norm, particularly when it comes to negative feedback. Here, uncertainty about people's reactions or fear that relationships might be damaged lead many managers to avoid giving feedback at all or to give feedback that is unclear and confusing. Lack of training in feedback techniques can also accentuate the problem.

CONSTRUCTIVE FEEDBACK CONVERSATIONS

EXAMPLE

Anil's managers always appeared supportive; he believed he was performing as expected. So he was surprised and upset when he found himself on a list of poor performers heading for redundancy when the company needed to reduce its headcount. Good intentions had avoided short-term pain, but longer-term all parties paid a high financial and emotional price.

To be fair, giving 'negative' feedback is daunting and it does not matter whether you present your feedback as 'constructive', 'negative' or 'developmental', if people perceive it as critical, or unfairly judgemental, they **will** react. One key reason is that people generally perceive themselves as doing a good job, so any feedback that challenges their world view will be an unwelcome surprise.

CONSTRUCTIVE FEEDBACK CONVERSATIONS

INFLUENCING REACTIONS

When your feedback surprises people, or is contrary to their frame of reference, they will naturally react with annoyance, frustration, verbal or passive anger. If you're seen as trying to be helpful, considerate and fair, however, your approach can influence short-term reactions and the long-term relationship. So you can dampen reactions and help focus attention on your feedback information by:

- Having helpful and constructive goals of your own
- Managing your expectations
- Being considerate to loss of face or embarrassment
- Setting the scene appropriately
- Being aware of defensive strategies
- Appreciating and working **with** the dynamics in the situation
- Knowing what to support and what to challenge

END GOALS

The goals with which you enter a feedback situation will shape your approach. For example, I've asked many managers their goals when giving feedback, and am often told: *'to get the person to change'* or *'to make them accept the feedback'*.

The managers are concentrating on what are known as 'end goals', where success is dependent on external uncontrollable factors going in their favour; for example, whether the other person accepts the feedback.

The more that is at stake, the more those end goals create the conditions for conflict or submission, because all parties may feel they'll lose face. A common end result is that someone appears to accept the feedback to escape the situation, but does not actually alter their subsequent performance.

CONSTRUCTIVE FEEDBACK CONVERSATIONS

A RANGE OF GOALS

To be helpful and constructive your goals need to aid, not escalate, the situation. One method is to have a range of goals to manage your expectations, focus your approach and review the success of the feedback conversation. For example:

- **The best possible end goal would be** – the feedback is accepted, acted on, and our feedback relationship develops further

- **A successful end goal would be** – the feedback is accepted, acted on, and their interest in feedback develops

- **An adequate end goal would be** – the feedback is acknowledged and not rejected, and trust increases

- **A failure would be** – the feedback is rejected and the relationship is damaged

CONSTRUCTIVE FEEDBACK CONVERSATIONS

PERSONAL PERFORMANCE GOALS

A further way to be constructive is to set yourself **performance** goals to help you reach your end goals. You achieve performance goals through controlling and managing your own behaviour. For example, *'To present my feedback clearly, explain why it is important to the business, listen to the response and engage in discussion and problem solving'*.
Or, *'Focus on making my feedback clear, appreciating they'll need to react, and maintaining the relationship'*.

Positive performance and end goals work together to support a helpful, constructive approach.

CONSTRUCTIVE APPROACH

A helpful, considerate and fair approach is also shaped by your language. The term 'negative feedback' creates all manner of expectations and attitudes in both feedback giver and receiver. It is challenging, emotive and tends to convey criticism more than development. At its worst, some managers use it as an excuse to be insensitive, find fault or demean.

An alternative approach is to find and use language for your feedback relationship that you all understand and are comfortable with. For example, some people I have worked with like the term 'constructive feedback', others prefer to use 'progressive feedback', others find the term 'feedforward' works for them. The key is to find and agree the words that work for both of you and that take the heat out of terms like 'negative feedback'.

CONSTRUCTIVE FEEDBACK CONVERSATIONS

MANAGING YOUR EXPECTATIONS

Like your goals, your expectations can inadvertently escalate sensitive situations. The following pages list six common ones to look out for and manage:

1. Don't expect people immediately to accept the feedback

People don't readily accept what they don't like or have no ownership of. The more negative, unjust or critical your feedback is perceived to be, the less accurate they believe it is; the more it challenges their world view, the more resistance they will have and the longer it will take them to accommodate the information.

To be helpful, consider the type of information that engages them. Do they respond to facts, statistics, emotional appeals? Consider whether the feedback should be 'drip fed', delivered over a series of meetings to help acceptance. But be aware that the latter approach might have a bad effect on morale if the process is not managed properly.

MANAGING YOUR EXPECTATIONS

2. Don't expect them to place the same importance on it as you do
Unless you've co-designed the feedback relationship, the feedback may be of little importance to them. Ask yourself why should they care? What's the WIIFM (what's in it for me) factor for them?

3. Don't expect people to be reasonable
Blame makes people defensive and words like *'you'* or *'your'* can convey blame, escalate the situation and reduce problem solving. For example, *'ten minutes more per customer could be used to show them the range'* is far more engaging than *'you always do the minimum with each customer'*.

MANAGING YOUR EXPECTATIONS

4. Don't expect them automatically to know what you're referring to
Length of time between incident and feedback is important. Leave it too long and people may forget the incident, or think you've stored a grudge. Perhaps the incident just wasn't important to them.

CONSTRUCTIVE FEEDBACK CONVERSATIONS

MANAGING YOUR EXPECTATIONS

5. Don't expect personal issues automatically to stay separate from performance issues

Differences between personal values can escalate a situation. Be aware of your own inferences and use objective data to manage yourself. Remember to be sensitive to the fact that people generally perceive that they are doing a good job.

6. Don't expect them to know what you want

It is surprising how many managers aren't clear about what they want. Your purpose is to develop future performance, so be clear about what the organisation needs. Try writing down what you need them to do differently and check it with people you trust. You'll be surprised how unclear you are initially.

CONSTRUCTIVE FEEDBACK CONVERSATIONS

SURPRISE, LOSS OF FACE OR EMBARRASSMENT

Being helpful and considerate can be demonstrated by the steps you take to minimise surprise, loss of face or embarrassment.

Surprises shouldn't happen; incremental development with agreed regular feedback is the best approach. But as the research (see page 92) highlighted, feedback is frequently avoided. Consider:

- **Setting/venue** – what is the most appropriate venue to minimise any loss of face?

- **During the conversation** emphasise your motives, clarify that you are not trying to embarrass or humiliate but value them and want to help them develop

- **Shock** – in some cases you may feel you want, or need, to shock someone to make them realise the seriousness of the situation. Consider the consequences and whether that is the only approach

CONSTRUCTIVE FEEDBACK CONVERSATIONS

SETTING UP THE CONVERSATION

When it comes to the actual feedback conversation you can be seen to be helpful, considerate and fair by clarifying your motives both to yourself and to the other person.

Clarify your role

Strange as it may seem, many managers I encounter haven't articulated clearly why they are responsible for feedback. Here are examples of how two different managers defined and legitimised their role and intentions:

'I am responsible for monitoring the overall profitability of the business and people's contributions in order to ensure profits and maintain jobs.'

'I am responsible for developing the skills of each person in my team so that in two years' time they can replace me in my job and I can progress.'

CONSTRUCTIVE FEEDBACK CONVERSATIONS

SETTING UP THE CONVERSATION

Other good techniques are:

Use objective measures. The more subjective your measures the more inaccurate your feedback will seem. Objective measures help focus attention away from personal areas. For example, a small business manager defined performance as 15% return above break even, and broke that into daily targets he could monitor so that he could give feedback on a weekly basis.

Take your time. Many managers rush into giving feedback and miss an opportunity to build trust and credibility by making their motives transparent. Take time to do this, by legitimising your role, and explaining the responsibilities that have compelled the feedback.

Use soft tactics initially. Joint problem solving, rationality, friendliness, desire to help performance, are all less likely to provoke strong reactions.

Challenge unacceptable standards. If their workplace behaviour has crossed acceptable lines then tell them so as early as possible in the feedback conversation.

CONSTRUCTIVE FEEDBACK CONVERSATIONS

PROTECTION STRATEGIES

Nobody likes being criticised so when someone perceives feedback as critical or negative it's only human to want to 'fight back'. Actual physical violence is rare but people will be inclined to use strategies to protect themselves. Some common approaches are to:

- Undermine the accuracy of your feedback, eg saying, *'But that is not what happened'*

- Cast doubt on your credibility/expertise: *'What would you know about the job I do?'*

- Cast doubt on your motives: *'You only give feedback when I have done something wrong'*

Reactions like these can be convincing because they are people's truths and it is easy to be drawn into a 'who is right?' argument. Stay above the argument and focus on your goals and objective data.

CONSTRUCTIVE FEEDBACK CONVERSATIONS

WORKING WITH THE DYNAMICS

Being determined to prove you are right and being determined to win can set the conditions for failure. Simmering resentment and feelings of injustice will drive people away from improving performance. It may be hard but:

Allow the reaction to run. Reactions and protection strategies do not go away. If closed down too quickly they'll be channelled into poor post-feedback performance. Give people time to react. Listen to them, let the heat dissipate, give them space to put forward their explanations.

Of course allowing a reaction to run is not easy. Your inclination, particularly if your values and expectations have been crossed, will be to defend or attack. Remember that reactions start as a physical sensation; learn to spot the early sensations so you're managing, rather than being driven by, your reactions.

CONSTRUCTIVE FEEDBACK CONVERSATIONS

WORKING WITH THE DYNAMICS

Try to distinguish between symptoms and causes. The magnifying glass effect naturally draws your attention to people and their behaviour. A consequence is that you might focus on symptoms rather than causes.

> **Example**
> Louis didn't generate enough income per customer. According to the manager Louis didn't allow enough time to offer the full range of products. However Louis worked alone with no role models, and had never been given any sales training. While the goals he worked towards were specific, his feedback was vague. Over time Louis had interpreted the job from his own frame of reference and had come to believe that technical skills were more important than sales skills.

Close a feedback conversation too quickly and you might only address symptoms. In Louis' case his manager's lack of contact had allowed him to form a deep seated belief that selling was not required. As hard as it sounds, try to keep the conversation open. Suspend judgement, enquire calmly to separate symptoms from causes, and listen for systems' causes, even if you don't like to hear them!

CONSTRUCTIVE FEEDBACK CONVERSATIONS

WORKING WITH THE DYNAMICS

When you are in the feedback conversation:

- **Acknowledge their effort**. If you forget to acknowledge the effort, or unique contribution, someone has made they are likely to become demotivated. Emphasise that the negative feedback is not a reflection of them as a person and that with support their skills will develop

- **Don't embed threats in the feedback**. When things aren't going as you want it is easy to react with threats. Use threats only when you have deliberately chosen to move to a harder approach

- **Forward focus**. If it is appropriate, move the conversation towards a forward focus: *'What are the next steps?'* and *'How can we develop the new performance?'*. With particularly challenging feedback, though, you might require a further meeting

WORKING WITH THE DYNAMICS

- **Is the problem with the person or with your feedback?** It can be easy to blame a poor outcome on the person: *'they wouldn't accept the feedback'*. However, sometimes the problem may be with your feedback or with how you delivered or interacted with the person concerned. If things haven't gone as you'd expected, step back, review your feedback and what happened. If the relationship between you is fundamentally sound, why not ask them what they thought happened or could be improved?

- **Apologise**. If you become aware that your feedback has hurt someone, apologise. It will build your credibility

Sorry!

CONSTRUCTIVE FEEDBACK CONVERSATIONS

SUPPORT & CHALLENGE

Within the feedback conversation there will be times to support and times to challenge performance. Support and challenge both help stimulate performance. However, too little support and too much challenge both lead to stress. Performance drops. With too much support and too little challenge, people will coast.

When things get heated, you may be tempted to drop your support and increase the challenge. This will lead to a build up of tension and undermine what you are trying to achieve, which is maintaining the relationship and encouraging acceptance of your feedback.

So in any feedback conversation, positive or negative, knowing what to support and what to challenge is critical for engaging motivation and development.

CONSTRUCTIVE FEEDBACK CONVERSATIONS

SUPPORT & CHALLENGE

Challenge underlying beliefs or attributions that might be barriers to performance. For example, *'I am a technician not a salesman'* indicates an underlying belief that you can question. You can say: *'It is not about selling, but about using those technical skills to give people good, attentive service and provide choice. They will choose what they want to buy from the range.'*

Support their ability to acquire skills. The acquisition of skills helps them grow in the job and can counter their underlying beliefs. For example, you can use reinforcing feedback: *'Well, you are already doing what is needed because 60% of the time you are on target. So you're not far off target and with support and ongoing feedback we can work together to enhance the skills you have'*. The conversation can progress to explore the best way to acquire the skills, for example training, mentoring, etc.

SUMMARY

The best way to manage feedback that may be perceived as negative is to have built an ongoing feedback relationship. As part of this, you will have agreed in advance how best to raise and deal with potential performance problems. If that relationship doesn't yet exist, and you need to give negative feedback:

Before

- Be timely so people can recall the issue under discussion

- Ensure you have objective measures and data, have process feedback prepared

- Appreciate them and their situation and consider how to minimise surprise or loss of face

- Be clear what your role and responsibilities are, making sure your goals and expectations are appropriate

CONSTRUCTIVE FEEDBACK CONVERSATIONS

SUMMARY (CONT'D)

During

- Set the scene – make your motives clear by legitimising your role and responsibility
- Be clear, specific and objective with your feedback, and focus on future performance that is controllable (focusing on the past is blame)
- Allow reactions and defensive strategies to dissipate, give the person space to explain
- Be open to generative feedback by being prepared to acknowledge and explore systems' causes

INTENTIONS INTO BEHAVIOUR

'I am sure of nothing so little as my own intentions.'

Lord Byron
Poet

INTENTIONS

People may genuinely intend to act on your feedback, but all manner of variables can undermine their efforts to turn intentions into behaviour. For one thing intentions are frail; just take the traditional New Year resolutions. Of thousands studied, in one piece of research, only 12% were successful.

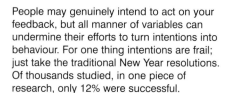

If intentions are to be successfully converted into behaviour they need support and strong belief.

INFLUENCES ON INTENTIONS

Intentions are influenced by:

- **Culture**. Culture is all pervasive; it shapes attitudes and behaviour yet is almost unnoticeable. It is conveyed by stories, power structures, systems, rituals, etc. Culture can discourage or encourage intentions. An enabling culture might support feedback conversations, reward development. A discouraging culture might hamper, restrict change

- **People**. The opinions and behaviour of family members, colleagues, managers and all the people you value and think credible are influential. The opinions of those people can sway, undermine or encourage intentions

STRENGTH OF BELIEF

To successfully make the journey from intention to behaviour a person needs:

- **Strength of belief**. New behaviour takes time, effort, commitment. For example, try to change a simple, ingrained habit such as how you wear a watch or tie your shoes. Without strength of belief, cultural norms will maintain the status quo, influential people will sway them off course, old habits remain and fresh demands distract focus and energy

- **Support**. Without support and encouragement people's tenacity will wane. If your feedback is to help intentions turn into performance then you need to support and nurture people as they make the attempt

INTENTIONS INTO BEHAVIOUR

CLARITY THROUGH GOALS

One way of offering support is by helping them be clear about their destination, which will help them maintain awareness and focus. You could encourage them to use **SMART goals**, which are **S**pecific, **M**easurable, **A**chievable, **R**ealistic, and **T**ime bound.

For example:
'Change the dry panel ordering system to save money' is vague.

While this is clearer:
'By the end of next week to have managed the procurement team review of the system for ordering dry panels and identified where 10% savings could be made and put together an outline plan for how the changes can be implemented.'

Not everyone, though, responds to **SMART** goals. Some people prefer what are called well formed outcomes, a picture of what success might look like, or the difference between OK performance and fantastic performance. If they are capable people they'll know what sort of goals work for them.

STRENGTHENING DESIRE

You can support people's strength of belief by building their **desire** to reach that final destination.

Desire is when the destination is important to them. It is linked to **their** aspirations, their developmental needs and goals. Desire comes when the WIIFM factor is high. If you've established an ongoing feedback relationship you'll be aware of their short- and long-term goals.

However, if your feedback lacks relevance or is imposed, it will be that much harder to support and strengthen their intentions; it may even be seen as a hindrance.

PUSH & PULL QUESTIONS

You can use coaching techniques to help people strengthen their **clarity** and **desire**. Questions that push or pull people can be helpful, for example:

- What do you want to achieve?
- On a scale of 1-10 how important is that to you?
- What would 'great' look like? What does 'fantastic' look like?
- What will it look like when you reach it?
- What would someone you really admire advise you to do?
- What will happen if you don't try?
- What have you got to lose?

INTENTIONS INTO BEHAVIOUR

ASK – OFFER – REVIEW

To master a new skill takes practice and commitment; indeed one study found people took anywhere from 18 to over 200 days to master new habits. No wonder people can run out of steam. Therefore ongoing support is crucial, particularly if the skill or behaviour is complex or abstract. The simplest way to provide support is to **Ask – Offer – Review**.

- **Ask** – co-design the ongoing relationship, clarifying the type, style and frequency of support they find works best for them

- **Offer** – many people find it difficult to ask for help; in addition they may not be aware of all the options available. You can suggest meeting at lunch breaks, possible training courses, a mentor

- **Review** – always conduct a quick review of the feedback conversation, levels of satisfaction and whether anything in the feedback agreement needs to change

SUMMARY

Remember!
- Manage your expectations; feedback affects intentions – not behaviour
- We all form intentions – whether they actually happen depends on people's strength of conviction and belief that **they can do** the behaviour
- Behaviour change doesn't occur overnight, it takes time!

Strength of conviction is needed to overcome influences
- Build a culture that encourages feedback and development
- Jointly identify goals to create a desire for something to aim for
- Use push and pull questions or **SMART** techniques to help people clarify their goals

Ask – Offer – Review
Build a strong ongoing feedback relationship by:
- Asking them and co-designing the feedback relationship
- Offering support with suggested mentors, meetings
- Reviewing the feedback relationship and progress on goals

FINAL WORDS

Regular feedback is one of your most critical management and relationship skills. If you make it a co-owned process acceptance will increase because it automatically becomes engaging, of value and use to the person. In addition remember:

Perception

● Manage your perception – appreciate people and their situation, use **SOLD** to reduce bias

Composing feedback

● Your feedback needs to be accurate, of value and use. Consider how you use the different types of feedback (outcome, process, comparative and evaluative); process feedback has the greatest developmental value

FINAL WORDS

Feedback conversations
- Jointly design the feedback relationship to make your feedback more relevant
- Work with the dynamic of the situation, listen as much as you talk, enquire, explore
- Support the development of skills – challenge inhibiting beliefs

Intentions into behaviour
- Build *desire* and *clarity* to strengthen intentions
- Ask – Offer – Review

Treat your staff in the way you expect them to treat your customers; what is good for a customer is good for business.

THE MANAGEMENT POCKETBOOK SERIES

Pocketbooks (also available in e-book format)

360 Degree Feedback
Absence Management
Appraisals
Assertiveness
Balance Sheet
Business Planning
Business Writing
Call Centre Customer Care
Career Transition
Coaching
Communicator's
Competencies
Creative Manager's
C.R.M.
Cross-cultural Business
Customer Service
Decision-making
Delegation
Developing People
Diversity
Emotional Intelligence
Employment Law
Empowerment
Energy and Well-being
Facilitator's
Feedback

Flexible Workplace
Handling Complaints
Icebreakers
Impact & Presence
Improving Efficiency
Improving Profitability
Induction
Influencing
International Trade
Interviewer's
I.T. Trainer's
Key Account Manager's
Leadership
Learner's
Management Models
Manager's
Managing Assessment Centres
Managing Budgets
Managing Cashflow
Managing Change
Managing Customer Service
Managing Difficult Participants
Managing Recruitment
Managing Upwards
Managing Your Appraisal
Marketing

Meetings
Mentoring
Motivation
Negotiator's
Networking
NLP
Nurturing Innovation
Openers & Closers
People Manager's
Performance Management
Personal Success
Positive Mental Attitude
Presentations
Problem Behaviour
Problem Solving
Project Management
Psychometric Testing
Resolving Conflict
Reward
Sales Excellence
Salesperson's
Self-managed Development
Starting In Management
Strategy
Stress
Succeeding at Interviews

Tackling Difficult Conversations
Talent Management
Teambuilding Activities
Teamworking
Telephone Skills
Telesales
Thinker's
Time Management
Trainer Standards
Trainer's
Training Evaluation
Training Needs Analysis
Virtual Teams
Vocal Skills
Working Relationships
Workplace Politics

Pocketfiles

Trainer's Blue Pocketfile of
Ready-to-use Activities

Trainer's Green Pocketfile of
Ready-to-use Activities

Trainer's Red Pocketfile of
Ready-to-use Activities

18.11.09

About the Author

Mike Pezet, BA Hons, MSc (Personal and Organisational Development).
Mike has been helping organisations and people develop their confidence and their ability to use feedback more effectively for over 15 years. For the last eight years he has worked extensively with leading UK and international companies, designing and delivering leadership programmes that are measured by bottom line results.

Mike is a trained coach, mediator and facilitator. He is interested in and welcomes feedback from those of you who wish to share any insights or stories from your use of this book, or your own feedback experiences.

Contact
You can email Mike via: info@feedbacktoolkit.com

Your details

Name _____

Position _____

Company _____

Address _____

_____

_____

Telephone _____

Fax _____

E-mail _____

VAT No. (EC companies) _____

Your Order Ref _____

Please send me:

	No. copies
The Feedback Pocketbook	
The _____ Pocketbook	
The _____ Pocketbook	
The _____ Pocketbook	

Order by Post
MANAGEMENT POCKETBOOKS LTD
LAUREL HOUSE, STATION APPROACH,
ALRESFORD, HAMPSHIRE SO24 9JH UK
Order by Phone, Fax or Internet
Telephone: +44 (0)1962 735573
Facsimile: +44 (0)1962 733637
E-mail: sales@pocketbook.co.uk
Web: www.pocketbook.co.uk

Customers in USA should contact:
Management Pocketbooks
2427 Bond Street, University Park, IL 60466
Telephone: 866 620 6944   Facsimile: 708 534 7803
E-mail: mp.orders@ware-pak.com
Web: www.managementpocketbooks.com

MANAGEMENT POCKETBOOKS